(from **WATT** *by Samuel Beckett, 1953)*

Watt now found himself in the midst of things which, if they consented to be named, did so as it were with reluctance. And the state in which Watt found himself resisted formulation in a way no state had ever done, in which Watt had ever found himself, and Watt had found himself in a great many states, in his day. Looking at a pot, for example, or thinking of a pot, at one of Mr Knott's pots, of one of Mr Knott's pots, it was in vain that Watt said, Pot, pot. Well, perhaps not quite in vain, but very nearly. For it was not a pot, the more he looked, the more he reflected, the more he felt sure of that, that it was not a pot at all. It resembled a pot, it was almost a pot, but it was not a pot of which one could say, Pot, pot, and be comforted. It was in vain that it answered, with unexceptionable adequacy, all the purposes, and performed all the offices, of a pot, it was not a pot. And it was just this hairbreadth departure from the nature of a true pot that so excruciated Watt. For if the approximation had been less close, then Watt would have been less anguished. For then he would not have said, This is a pot, and yet not a pot, but then he would have said, This is something of which I do not know the name. And Watt preferred on the whole having to do with things of which he did not know the name . . .

(from **BIRD LIVES!** *by Ross Russell, 1972)*

The *Klactoveesedstene* title was Charlie Parker's own. He wrote it out one night at the Deuces on the back of a minimum charge card, offering no explanation of its meaning. When I asked, he gave me a stony stare and walked off. Was it a person, a place, an abstract idea, or a new entry in the jive lexicon? After consulting the large desk model of Webster's and after that Skeat's Etymological Dictionary, both without result, I asked a psychiatrist if she could help. She could not. I then consulted Dean Benedetti, who pointed out at once what to him was quite obvious: "*Klactoveesedstene? Why, man, it's just a sound.*"

The POT! (Poetry Olympics Twenty05) Anthology
Edited by Michael Horovitz
New Departures #36–37

Published in 2005 by New Departures
PO Box 9819, London W11 2GQ
info@poetryolympics.com

Design by Frazzlefish with Michael Horovitz

Inside covers – 'Picture-Poem #68: Serpentine–Elephantine–TURPENTINE!' (Michael Horovitz)
This page – Photograph of Allen Ginsberg at RAH, 1965 (John Goldblatt)

A CIP catalogue record for this book is available from the Britsish Library.

ISBN 0 902689 25 8

Contents / Picture credits

Acknowledgements

Heartfelt thanks to each artist, writer, photographer and cartoonist, living and dead, whose work is reproduced in this collection – and also to their editors, publishers, executors, managers and agents. And specifically, to:

SAMUEL BECKETT and Calder Publications, for the excerpt from *Watt*, 1958

ROSS RUSSELL and Quartet Books for the excerpt from *Bird Lives!*, 1972

CHRISTOPHER LOGUE and Faber & Faber, for 'Professor Tucholsky's Facts' in *Selected Poems* 1996, and for the excerpt from *Prince Charming*, 1999

LIBBY HOUSTON and Slow Dancer Press, for 'Post-War' from *Cover of Darkness*, 1999 – and also to Libby for the late Mal Dean's drawings of her and Roger McGough made in 1966

EDWIN MORGAN and Carcanet, for his Ode 'For the First International Poetry Incarnation' in *Collected Poems*, 1990

ALLEN GINSBERG, City Lights and Viking for 'Studying the Signs' from *Collected Poems*, 1985; again to Ginsberg and Penguin Books for 'Graphic Winces', in *Cosmopolitan Greetings*, 1994

LAWRENCE FERLINGHETTI and City Lights for 'London Crossfigured' in *Pictures of the Gone World*, 1955

JOE PAICE and Haunted Ballroom for 'Greasy Spoon' from the album *A Man and his Dream* 2005

SLIM GAILLARD and the Hep Label's *McVouty*, *Slim Gaillard: The Voutest*, and other classic Slim recordings, for 'Matzoh Balls' and 'Cement Mixer'

LINTON KWESI JOHNSON, LKJ Music Publishing Ltd and Bloodaxe Books, for 'Reggae Sounds' in *Tings an Times* 1991

SUJATA BHATT and Carcanet for 'Phytoremediation' from her forthcoming collection

ADRIAN MITCHELL and Bloodaxe Books for 'William Blake Says: Every Thing That Lives Is Holy' and 'Work To Do' in *The Shadow Knows: Poems 2000–2004*, 2004

WALLY FAWKES aka TROG, Telegraph Newspapers and The Centre for the Study of Cartoons and Caricature, University of Kent, for 'Neo-Crusaders', which first appeared in the Sunday Telegraph on 14 November 2004

STEVE BELL for 'Dog on the Couch', first published in The Guardian, 8 June 2005

GRACE NICHOLS and Virago, for 'Our Cassandra' in *Startling the Flying Fish*, forthcoming

PETE TOWNSHEND and Eel Pie Publishing Ltd for *Wake Up And Hear The Music* 2005 and *In the Ether* 2004

RACHEL FULLER, Universal Records and Eel Pie for 'Cigarettes and Housework' and 'Around This Table' on *Cigarettes and Housework* 2005

STEVIE SMITH and The Estate of James MacGibbon for 'Not Waving but Drowning' and the three Stevie drawings (the two with her handwritten remarks were featured in *Some Are More Human Than Others*, first published by Gaberbocchus Press in 1958, and republished by Peter Owen in 1990)

JOHN HEGLEY and Methuen, for the two poems and Joseph drawing in *Love Cuts*, 1995

FRANCES HOROVITZ, Enitharmon Press, Bloodaxe Books and Roger Garfitt, for 'Walking in Autumn' from *Water Over Stone* 1980 and *Collected Poems* 1985

KATHRYN WILLIAMS, Neil le Flohic, Warner Chappell Publishing and Caw Records Ltd, for 'Old Low Light #2' and 'Beachy Head' from *Over Fly Over* 2005; 'Stevie' will be on her next album

Sophie Parkin

Adam Horovitz
Stevie Smith
Grace Nichols

Neil Sparkes
Roger McGough
John Agard

This Miscellany is partly a hymn book to back up and survive the Poetry Olympics Twenty05 (POT!) Festival which consists of two events, one at London's Royal Albert Hall on 25 September '05, and the other at The 100 Club (100 Oxford St) on October 6.

The Albert Hall event was conceived as a 'Forty Years After / *Wholly Communion* Renewed', to revisit and replenish the sense of connection and liberation that swirled around Britain in the wake of the First International Poetry Incarnation. This gig filled the Hall to overflowing in the Summer of 1965, attracting the largest audience for public poetry in the UK in living or recorded memory.

The Times Literary Supplement of 17 June '65 devoted a full-page leader to the gathering and concluded that it "made literary history by a combination of flair, courage and seized opportunities".

I jotted some perhaps over-rhapsodic reflections on my sense of what happened that evening, and what it betokened, in my editorial 'Afterword' to *Children of Albion: Poetry of the Underground in Britain* (Penguin 1969 – pages 336 & *ff*). Many changes have taken place around poetry since 1965 and one purpose of this Anthology, as of the POT! events, is to illustrate those changes and prime a fresh and positive canvas for the decades to come, rather than revel in the high times some of us had in the Sixties.

As well as the original megagig's 40th anniversary, this festival and booklet also celerate the 25th birthday of Poetry Olympics, which my friends and I launched at Westminster Abbey on Friday 26th September 1980. Twenty05 is also my own 70th birthday year. So – with unseemly if characteristic immodesty – I have featured quite a lot of pieces of my own manufacture, alongside several salutations kind friends have composed in my honour. Many thanks to each of these (and apologies to readers with little appetite for the Festshcrift mode).

There is much else here, however. Plenty of inspiring new blood. Plenty of laughs and sounds. Plenty plenty soul, anti-war and radical vision.

The 1965 RAH poetmeet presented seventeen white males (from eight countries) plus guitarist Davey Graham. The two main developments in English-speaking verse I've observed, promoted and delighted in since then are, the continuing participation in our shared poetic community by non-white and women writers, performers and auditors. And equally, the continuing productive interplay and overlaps between poetry, music and song. I hope that you will relish as much as I do the diverse examples I've trawled from these far-flowing springs.

I have also committed plenty of space to mark the passing of seminal accomplices – the most recently departed having been mainstays of the New Departures/Jazz Poetry SuperJam road-shows: Jeff Nuttall and Dick Heckstall-Smith. Both were remarkable team players whose knack for bringing extremely unlikely fellow artists and musos together will be much missed by everyone who enjoyed the stimulus of their flamboyant energies over the years.

Dick, the multi-saxophone colossus, who left us on 17 December '04, had been one of the first and foremost UK jazz poetry engineers, with Pete Brown, myself and others, from 1959 until cancer forced him to stop playing in 2001. You can get the tenor of his tenor on characteristically exuberant form – simultaneously subtle and barnstorming – on 'Tin Roof Blues' from a SuperJam at The 100 Club in 1996 (Track 15 of *Jeff Nuttall's Wake on CD* – see page 110), building to an orgasmic climax whilst holding together the various styles of Pete on drums, Jeff's red-hot cornet, rockette Andi Kay on bass, Ian Smith's lovely bit of trumpet and my sub-Red McKenziean kazoo. And Dick's saxes are equally potent reinforcing Neil Sparkes's jazz and blues poems on the *Grandchildren of Albion Live* recordings (see page 111).

My thanks to all the poets, singer-songwriters, artists and photographers who have contributed their produce so generously to fill and enrich this POT!

There follows a Vox Pop from some of the protagonists of the 1965 incarnation, beginning with the Invocation some ten of our 'Poets' Co-operative' improvised amidst the Rizlas, joss sticks & beatnik squalor of Alex Trocchi's basement in St. Stephen's Gardens, Notting Hill all those cool and crazy (– sometimes all too crazy) years ago:

> World declaration hot peace shower! Earth's grass is
> free! Cosmic poetry Visitation accidentally happening
> carnally! Spontaneous planet-chant Carnival! Mental
> Cosmonaut poet-epiphany, immaculate supranational
> Poesy insemination!
>> Skullbody love-congress Annunciation,
> duende concordium, effendi tovarisch illumination,
> Now! Sigmatic New Departures Residu of Better
> Books & Moving Times in obscenely New Directions!
> Soul revolution City Lights Olympian lamb-blast!
> Castalia centrum new consciousness hungry
> generation Movement roundhouse 42 beat
> apocalypse energy-triumph!
>> You are not alone!
> Miraculous assumption! O Sacred Heart invisible
> insurrection! Albion! awake! awake! awake! O
> shameless bandwagon! Self-evident for real naked
> come the words! Global synthesis habitual for this
> Eternity! Nobody's Crazy Immortals Forever!

ALEXANDER TROCCHI: One might say it was in the air, has been since after 1945, this felt need on the part of poets, artists, thinking individuals in general for a coming together internationally of individuals in an immediate way, transcending politics. In another place, I called this growing protest and the various calls for some kind of direct action the "invisible insurrection", and I argued that at its most articulate, this (r)evolt is against the whole gamut of traditional response which is unconscious for the most part, hallowed by convention, and quite inadequate for the complex world which has been thrust upon us by the relentless evolution of our own technology. During the last two decades there have been many international cultural festivals, but this manifestation at the Royal Albert is remarkable in that, conceived, plotted, and undertaken in ten short days, the thousands came and many were turned away at the door.

The impulse to bring all these people together to participate in an evening of poetry was regarded by some of us as a kind of experiment in human festival, a practical demonstration of the immediate availability of creative people of very different backgrounds to the idea of cultural experiment. And the toleration they showed of some very indifferent poetry during more than four hours was surely evidence of the audience's general appreciation that something was being achieved, something significant and to do with human solidarity, just by our all being there at all in such a place, poets so very different, all together, participating. This concordium was above all a happening, conceived joyfully and seriously in the spirit of play. The idea caught on, the various poets boarded the "shameless bandwaggon" (cf. programme notes), and set about demonstrating that the greatest concert-hall in England was hardly big enough to contain all those who, at the shortest notice, would come from all over in answer to this spontaneous gesture of international goodwill. For myself, I think it is not so much a question of choosing to co-operate as of discovering oneself in and of the "invisible insurrection" by virtue of one's practical posture. The (r)evolt is taking place at the level of symbols: there is no question of our ever meeting the forces of reaction head on in a war on their terms. But it is happening. If you are aware of it, you are *ipso facto* involved. To quote again from the programme notes: "Self-evident for real naked come the words . . ."

(from Feliks Topolski's *Chronicle,* Vol XIII 1965)

SPIKE HAWKINS: The Albert Hall was a surging thing. I read a few small things. It was very exciting being led along by Pete Brown and Horovitz, and I said 'Where do we go?' and they took me down to this tunnel and it was very badly lit, and suddenly this lid went up and I found myself with the light of the world upon me, and thousands of people, just coming out of this little hole in the ground over the stage. I felt this must be some sort of metaphor. I was totally astounded by it.

(from Days In The Life, ed. Jonathon Green, Cape 1986)

ADRIAN MITCHELL: There's a natural hunger for poetry in everyone. But the invention of printing & glum-headed education managed to cut poems down to dwarf size. Poetry eating became a solitary, rare and almost perverted occupation. In this century people became so jumpy they could hardly nibble. But one by one & four by four, poets broke out of their cells. Edith Sitwell tried. Dylan Thomas made it and was punished to death. Ginsberg and Ferlinghetti and Yevtushenko opened the gates and out we rushed, blinking and drinking in the light. In the past five, six, seven years more and more British poets have been stomping the island giving adrenaline transfusions in cellars, town halls, schools, clubs, pubs, theatres, anywhere. Whenever enough people knew that poetry was around they came, grabbed it and started chewing. So it's no surprise that 7,000 plus came to the Albert Hall feast. It wasn't the beginning of anything, it was public proof of what had been accelerating for years ... I want poetry to bust down all the walls of its museum tomb and learn to survive in the corrosive real world. The walls are thick, but a hundred Joshuas are on the job. Some of them were at the Albert Hall.

(*from Children of Albion*, ed. Michael Horovitz, Penguin 1969)

JEFF NUTTALL: I was going to perform a happening with John Latham, and he covered himself with blue paint and this blocked his pores and he passed out. And he had to be put in a bath. I had funny paint on as well and I got in the bath with him. The caretaker, who was outraged by whoever these people were who had taken over the Albert Hall, came into the dressing-room suspecting that drugs were being smoked. 'What's going on 'ere?' — and people giggled cos they were stoned out of their heads. Then he burst into the bathroom and said, 'Oh my Gawd, oh my Gawd!' and went.

I didn't read myself, but I heard the readings. It was superb. Ginsberg was wonderful, Ferlinghetti too — all the professional rhetorical readers were very good indeed ... All our separate audiences came to one place at the same time, a frisson for us all to savour as there had been at the first Aldermaston, and the underground was suddenly there on the surface, in open ground with a following of thousands.

(*from Days In The Life*, ed. Jonathon Green, Cape 1986)

ERNST JANDL: No-one was one, but we each were the thousands, re-shaped in one beautiful body of voices and echoes, with Allen Ginsberg on our soul.

Common Market

The old trench coat
searches for a trench
under the haystacks
in Europe

Respect

Respect the dandy lion.
He is the joker
on your path.
In childhood
We blew him hard
to find the time.
The strict gardener
called him a gypsy
of the lawn.
I often wish
as I blow
their parachutes
                somewhere,
nowhere.
          A clock
and vagabond. Blow
safely yellow
and his seeds will
return to the sun
all your unsaid
secrets.
          Step
gently.

Warrants

Policemen are numbered
for only one reason

In case they get lost.

Found
in the top hat

I found the girl behind
the smoking mirrors
and Chinese whispers.
We went to bed
to pursue new arrangements
in positions never put
to paper.

Dear Mr Bush

A smart bomb
would stay
at home!

Professor Tucholsky's Facts

Once upon a little planet,
a neat, provincial planet, set
deep in the galactic sticks,
there lived an interesting thing
called *Man*.

Man had two legs, and two *Convictions*:
one was called *Luck*,
which he described as *Good* when things went *Right*.
The other one he used when things went *Wrong*.
This was called *Religion*.

Man was vertebrate, bipedic, often bald,
and had a *Soul* that never died.
Also – to check his overconfidence –
he had his *Leaders*, and his *Fellow Countrymen*.

Man ate a lot:
plants, fish, animals, birds, snails . . .
in fact, he ate whatever he could kill.
Occasionally he ate his *Fellow Man* –
but this was rare.

Each man had a liver, a heart, a brain,
and a *Flag*.
These were his vital organs.
On these his life depended.

I have no doubt that there were men alive
with only half a liver;
some had no heart;
and many had no brain.
But a man without a flag?
Impossible!

Man was the most *Useful* of earthly creatures.
Cheerfully he raised the value of shares,
cheerfully he died a soldier's death,
or committed spectacular crimes –
thereby selling innumerable newspapers
all of which have now vanished.

Many admired *Human Character* –
but it was split.
One half was known as *Male*
and did not want to think:
the other half was known as *Female*,
in whom thinking was discouraged.

Yet both had this in common:
they were full of fear.
They were afraid of death, of debt,
of loneliness, of failure, and of war.
But most of all they feared their *Fellow Man*.

Of course, some men were different:
Thinkers, or *Revolutionaries*, or *Saints*.
However, these were few; and they
were quickly crucified, or shot, or poisoned.

Next week we study Dogs.

Occasionally, interesting events materialise from a general mood. One person says to another: 'Let's do so-and-so,' and things begin to move.

The Albert Hall poetry reading of 11 June 1965 was like this. Alex called. Realising there were a number of American and European poets in London, he and Michael Horovitz had formed a Poets' Co-operative to plan a large public reading.

(l to r: Michael Horovitz, John Esam, Harry Fainlight, Lawrence Ferlinghetti, Alex Trocchi, Allen Ginsberg, Simon Vinkenoog, Dan Richter, Julie Felix, early June 1965)

'We met in Trocchi's flat,' Michael said. 'The Americans – Corso, Ferlinghetti, Ginsberg – were reading here and there in London, all seats sold. Then we heard that Andrei Voznesensky, the Austrian sound-poet Ernst Jandl, Simon Vinkenoog and Anselm Hollo were in town, with Pablo Neruda expected. "What is the biggest hall in London?" The Albert Hall. Free in ten days' time. A £600 bond for the day.'

Jill Richter, the wife of Daniel – he choreographed and led the hominidae sequences at the beginning of *2001* – put up the money, and during those ten days the Co-operative covered the town with publicity. Better Books sold out of tickets. 'Still,' Alex said 'we were nervous. We had sold 500 tickets at five shillings and ten shillings each. 500 people are lost in the Albert Hall.'

To promote sales, Alex suggested holding a press conference on the steps of the Albert Memorial. Everyone turned up: Ginsberg, with Harry Fainlight dancing around him, Simon wearing glasses with sunflowers painted on the lenses,

Michael Horovitz, Julie Felix, Ferlinghetti, Barry and Sue Miles, surrounded by a fantastically dressed, handsome collection of obviously happy young men and women. All this to the delight of a BBC-TV outside broadcast unit that delivered enough good material for the nine o'clock news to include a minute-long item on the conference, with full details of the First Great International Poetry Reading about to be held at the Royal Albert Hall, announced in the sunshine by Alex in his caftan.

I had put the date of the reading in my diary, and forgotten about it. I missed the press conference, but saw it broadcast, wishing I had been there. I was sure that it would add at least two thousand to the number of tickets already sold.

The weather had held. About 6.30 p.m. I walked up to the Gate, then, in the warm evening light, across the park to Kensington Gore with some of my poems in a folder. There were a few people buying tickets at the outside box-office. A doorman directed me to the artists' entrance - my first time behind the scenes in this famous building. Another doorman had my name on his list of readers.

Good old Alex. In I went.

Simon's was the first known face I saw. 'This way,' he said, in a serious tone.

We went through a tunnel. Seconds later, we stepped into the light of this vast domed space where thousands of faces looked down on us, breathtaking banks of them, filling the Hall – a place intended for the performance of works of enduring beauty – itself suffused with a light that was like candlelight in its effect, though stronger, while here and there, a spot travelled over the audience – a sight that drew a silent gasp from me, as had my first visit to the British Library's round reading room.

Between seven and eight thousand people had come. Photographs show the Hall full. Helpers brought what remained of the stock from the Covent Garden flower market As the audience arrived, they were given daffodils, tulips, roses and greenery. People sat where they chose. "You sensed expectancy," Alex said. 'We were astonished. Delighted. The evening centred on the poets. We half-emptied the arena' – the Hall's central floor space – 'of seats and arranged a horseshoe of tables set with water and wine for the readers. At the middle of the space was a low, microphoned podium, beside it a high stool with lectern and a second microphone.' From which Alex, as master of ceremonies, announced each reader.

At Alex's flat, the Co-operative had composed an Invocation beginning with a quotation from Blake's 'Jerusalem':

> 'England! awake! awake! awake!
> Jerusalem thy Sister calls!'

      *   *   *

> And now the time returns again:
> Our souls exult, & London's towers
> Receive the Lamb of God to dwell
> In England's green & pleasant bowers.'

So the evening began.

My awe was warmed by the happy buzz rising and falling as Alex called poet after poet to the stand, detaching the microphone from the neck of the one departing, attaching it with a 'Don't be too long now', to the next.

For me – perhaps only for me – to see my now distant friend Alex as his early 1950s' self again was a boon. Relaxed, confident, humorous, very much in charge. As the press said: 'A model chairman, introducing the speakers without fuss and exercising a kindly but implacable "guillotine" when the minutes allowed for each poet were up'. It was the moment that spoke. A big, discrete, concentrated, four-hour moment, wishing poetry well in the city that had sheltered a number of its fairest voices.

(Michael Horovitz, Alex Trocchi, Pete Brown, Daniel Richter)

For me, the high point of the Albert Hall event – it can be seen in the video of *Wholly Communion*, Peter Whitehead's film of the reading – was the performance of Kurt Schwitters' sound poem, '*The Furore of Sneezing*', by Pete Brown, Jandl and Horovitz. The text (or score?) of the poem goes:

> *Tesch, Haisch, Tschiiaa*
> *Haisch, Tschiiaa*
> *Haisch, Happaisch*
> *Happapeppaisch*
> *Happapeppaisch*
> *Happapeppaisch*
> *Happapeppaisch*
> *Happa peppe*
>
> *TSCHAA!*

(*Ernst Jandl, Michael Horovitz, Pete Brown*)

... which the trio, led by Jandl – a superb verbal technician – gave in about a minute. Starting:

> '*Tesch ... Haisch ... Tschiiaa ...*'

the suspense rising through:

> '*Haisch, Happaisch ...*'

to the almost unbearable:

> '*Happa ... peppe ...*'

all 8,000 of us dying for the release of

> '*TSCHAA!*'

Ginsberg was the star. As much a priest, a rabbi, as a poet. By any standard, an impressive man at the height of his reputation, surrounded by those he inspired, he shuffled away under a cloud of thrown rose leaves as the show came to a close.

(— from 'Prince Charming: A Memoir' by Christopher Logue, Faber and Faber 1999)

im anfang war das wort
('in the beginning was the word')

him hanfang war das wort hund das wort war bei
gott hund gott war das wort hund das wort hist fleisch
geworden hund hat hunter huns gewohnt

him hanflang war das wort hund das wort war blei
flott hund flott war das wort hund das wort hist fleisch
gewlorden hund hat hunter huns gewlohnt

schim schanflang war das wort schund das wort war blei
flott schund flott war das wort schund das wort schist
fleisch gewlorden schund schat schunter schuns gewlohnt

schim schanschlang schar das wort schlund schasch wort
schar schlei schlott schund flott war das wort schund
schasch fort schist schleisch scheschlorden schund
schat schlunter schluns scheschlohnt

s——— c———h
s——— c———h
schills ——— c———h
flottsch

schützengraben
(the trenches)

schtzngrmm
schtzngrmm
t – t – t – t
t – t – t – t
grrrmmmmm
t – t – t – t
s ———— c ———— h
tzngrmm
tzngrmm
tzngrmm
grrrmmmmm
schtzn
schtzn
t – t – t – t
t – t – t – t
schtzngrmm
schtzngrmm
tssssssssssss sss
grrt
grrrrrt
grrrrrrrrrt
scht
scht
t – t – t – t – t – t – t – t – t
scht
tzngrmm
tzngrmm
t – t – t – t – t – t – t – t – t
scht
scht
scht
scht
scht
grrrrrrrrrr rrrrrrrrr
t – tt

Post-War

In 1943
my father
dropped bombs on the continent

I remember
my mother
talking about bananas
in 1944

when it rained,
creeping alone to the windowsill,
I stared up the hill,
watching, watching,
watching without a blink
for the Mighty Bananas
to stride through the blitz

they came in paper bags
in neighbours' hands
when they came
and took their time
over the coming

and still I don't know
where my father
flying home
took a wrong turning

A walk through the old sketchbook:
Ladbroke Grove, '64

Evening.
Raining.
Gentle.
    Air unholylit as if the dawn this
       dawn of night
           a flood of pallor

Sky
       pavementstreaked
Pavement
       skygrained
Trees hiding their green in houses
Applecore swiftly turning
     roadgrey   in the gutter

Far off
drab
streetlines
     moving suddenly into people!
       people shapes
   shifting into walls
         faces
    bent over in yellow windows

The leaning bus drawn at the drainside
         dark blue men lingering

Rain.
Tender.
    (mother   lover)
Rain.
smoothing red blue black
umbrellas' humped backs
my brow's
     clamped rigs

Notting Hill Carnival Poem*

A pageant of floating foliage
beating conga drums and dustbin lids
with clarion pipes and wild smoke paint
and fancy dress stirs joy
enough to get
          policemen even
                dancing
up the Grove – O *rittum*, the rhythm
joins peaceloving light-
and dark-skinned hands
and hearts and heads and bands
       in jumping jubilee –
grabbing great branches, a shuffling swaying
triumphal march in glad hurrah – *every-*
body do dis t'ing
– children – all ages
chorusing – 'We all live
       in a *yellow* submarine'
– trumpeting tin bam good-time stomp –
a sun-smiling wide-open steelpan-chromatic
neighbourhood party making love not war
– and the televisions all around
     have closed their electronic eyes
         knocked out by spontaneous reality
now autumn welcomes you to spring
in Notting Hill,
       where universe collides
with universe, and still
   nothing gets broken

* This was written at the first Notting Hill Carnival in August 1966, which was a relatively small-scale revival of the pre-war Notting Hill Fayre, set up by a multiracial group of community-minded local residents; essentially it was just a summer festival street-party. Over the years the event has tended to get aggrandised, congested, over-amplified, and sometimes spoiled by a tiny fraction of nasties, or by the conflicting vested interests of non-celebrants. Nevertheless:

'. . . Lawd, don' stop the Carnival!'

Michael Horovitz

......fresh flowers surrounded us

the bright young men
poised at the microphone
night after   errant night
pointing lips to a mouthburst
would shimmer through   mind-ceilings
blast the corners off   every square
enclosed   inch   of cerebration
swing it   gently into   celebration
of the glorious dream   beauty
human kind   quested   ever since   time
interceded   its paralysing   prison
laws   of moral punctuation
I'm still conscious of   ignoring
now is why   i confess myself
still subject   to inexorable
guillotine   curtains
intimations   of mortality
last gasps   on parole
so dance your dance   eternal death
but stay home   why don't you
leave us   alone   together
singing   for only   each other
to hear   till our mutual   ear
and tongues   give over
tired   of symbols   and turn
on   to love   only
turn on   to love

From **Mutation of the Spirit**

The decencies of life have lost their way
Tamarinds seek phalangers to flay
Green-thumbed spayers of dacthal
Scampering vermin
Darkness with all its failure annunciations stills the transept
Chip chip ecclesiastics aggregate in rhythmic throngs
Gods collide and eclipse the sick sun
What's seen What's seen
Eyes to the source and rinsed light between
Look upon look the great secret deep seen
Oracle and dial wand and radar
An angel comes and the new sun is not far
Arise new spirit unroll a nadir wool
From tip to top the source is measured full
The eternal exists as well in the ephemeral
Air is everywhere and life is changeable
In the yard of the old sun retired spirits sleep
Into the pool of night the swimmer of light leaps

For the International Poetry Incarnation
Royal Albert Hall, 11 June 1965

Worldscene! Worldtime! Spacebreaker! Wildship! Starman!
Gemini man dangles white and golden – the world floats
on a gold cord and curves blue white beautiful below him –
Vostok shrieks and prophesies, Mariner's prongs flash –
to the wailing of Voskhod Earth sighs, she shakes men loose at last –
out, in our time, to be living seeds sent far beyond
even imagination, though imagination is awake – take
poets on your voyages! Prometheus
embraces Icarus and in a gold shell with wings
he launches him up through the ghostly detritus
of gods and dirty empires and dying laws,
he mounts, he cries, he shouts, he shines, he streams
like light new done, his home is in a sun
and he shall be the burning unburned one.
In darkness, Daedalus
embraces Orpheus, the dark lips caked with earth and roots
he kisses open, the cold body he rubs
to a new life – the dream
flutters in a cage of crumbling bars, reviving

and then beginning slowly singing of the stars.

Beginning singing, born to go.
To cut the cord of gold. To get
the man new born to go.

Before You Sleep
(written after the Albert Hall poetry reading, June 1965)

move over and I'll tell you why
the poets won't bring revolutions
of love and flowers and poetry:

it's because most poets are egotists,
gross egotists, who are really a bit sad
that other poets exist

but are glad so many flowers exist
to pour out sutras and elegies over
and prove this poet's so good
he can even match the beauty of a flower

and glad of course that poetry was around
when they discovered that after all
they would not make it as a philosopher
or a holyman or a jazz musician or a painter
or the mightiest lover or the politician

poetry was around to sustain them
with the power dreams proffered
by the word

Move closer and I'll tell you about the poet
who was always writing love poems about his marvels
with his angel woman in bed:

you know, all the time he was writing
she was making it with a store detective.

£ S D

**(love, sex, death
pounds, shillings, pence
lysergic acid)**

Iron leaves gliint
where wind broke in,
red rot in rain:
my death is lead,
cloven by slow,
radium-sharp shark-fin.

In my soft tree-bole
bleeds pearl,
spreads spoor
of wee, unhungering,
ceaseless vole.

An end to blue and green
and tune;
no more delight
in the black cave
of your feminine night:

the poor silt of my years
is thin to spread ...
after I am dead, 'Margarine',
it will be said,
'he mistook it for butter'.

An end to sun,
moon, sky,
no young girl now will lie
in hot halter
of a pregnancy.

... young witches,
old bitches,
silvered resilience
of stagelit thighs,
hot, husky cries,
mascaraed eyes,
all manner of highs,
excruciatingly artificial.

Few virtues,
threadbare ascription ...
clues: blues
        cruise
        unpaid dues;
... dropped Plato
like a hot potato;
wouldn't work:
hashish of the Turk ...

There was a door between
him and himself.
Out, like the biff-ball
from the bat,
the limit taut,
feet sunk in cement,
tripped over himself,
a closing hinge:
himself something
upon which he couldn't impinge.

The Man and the Moon

The night tinkles
a chromium cash register
the little balls are orderly in their slots
cats laugh, their pointed teeth
the Sisters of Mercy furl their nets

Who can penetrate his own midnight?
Curb the insectal sputter of his own silences
while that great yellow gob, the moon
a jaundiced eye
shouts up at his shanks from the wet streets?

Studying the Signs

(After reading Basil Bunting's 'Briggflats')

White light's wet glaze on asphalt city floor,
the *Guiness Time* house clock hangs sky misty,
yellow *Cathay* food lamps blink, rain falls
on rose neon *Swiss Watch* under Regent archway,
Sun Alliance and London Insurance Group stands
granite–"Everybody gets torn down" . . . as a high
black taxi with orange doorlight passes around
iron railing blazoned with red sigma *Underground*–
Ah where the cars glide slowly around Eros
shooting down on one who stands in Empire's Hub
under his shining silver breast, look at Man's
sleepy face under half-spread metal wings–
Swan & Edgar's battlement walls the moving Circus,
princely high windows barred (shadow bank
interior office stairway marble) behind castiron
green balconies emblemed with single swans afloat
like white teacups what–*Boots'* blue sign lit up
over an enamel weight-machine's mirror clockface
at door betwixt plateglass *Revlon* & slimming biscuit
plaques and that alchemical blood-crimson pharmacy
bottle perched on street display. *A Severed Head*
"relished uproariously" above the masq'd *Criterion*
marquee, with Thespis and Ceres plaster Graces lifting
white arms in the shelled niches above a fire gong
on the wooden-pillared facade whose mansard gables
lean in blue-black sky drizzle, thin flagpole.
Like the prow of a Queen Mary the curved building
sign *Players* package, blue capped center
Navvy encircled by his life-belt a sweet bearded
profile against 19th century sea waves–
last a giant red delicious *Coca-Cola* signature
covers half the building back to gold *Cathay*.
Cars stop three abreast for the light, race forward,
turtleneck youths jump the fence toward *Boots*,
the night-gang in Mod slacks and ties sip
coffee at the *Snac-A-Matic* corner opendoor,
a boy leaned under *Cartoon Cinema* lifts hand
puffs white smoke and waits agaze–a wakened
pigeon flutters down from streetlamp to the fountain,
primly walks and pecks the empty pave–now deep
blue planet-light dawns in Piccadilly's low sky.

June 12, 1965

Graphic Winces

In highschool when you crack your front tooth bending down too fast
        over the porcelain water fountain

or raise the tuna sandwich to your open mouth and a cockroach tickles
        your knuckle

or step off the kitchen cabinet ladder on the ball of your foot hear the
        piercing meow of a soft kitten

or sit on a rattling subway next the woman scratching sores on her legs,
        thick pus on her fingers

or put your tongue to a winter-frozen porch door, a layer of frightening
        white flesh sticks to the wooden frame –

or pinch your little baby boy's fat neck skin in the last teeth of his
        snowsuit zipper

or when you cross Route 85 the double yellow line's painted over a dead
        possum

or tip your stale party Budweiser on the windowsill to your lips, taste
        Marlboro butts floating top of the can –

or fighting on the second flight of the tenement push your younger
        sister down the marble stairs she bites her tongue in half, they
        have to sew it back in the hospital –

or at icebox grabbing the half-eaten Nestlé's Crunch a sliver of foil
        sparks on your back molar's silver filling

or playing dare in High School you fall legs split on opposite sides of a
        high iron spiked fence

or kicked in the Karate Dojo hear the sound like a cracked twig then feel
        a slow dull throb in your left forearm,

or tripping fall on the sidewalk & rip last week's scab off your left knee

You might grimace, a sharp breath from the solar plexus, chill spreading
        from shoulderblades and down the arms,

or you may wince, tingling twixt sphincter and scrotum a subtle electric
        discharge.

December 8, 1986

(*Allen Ginsberg in his birthday suit at his 39th birthday party in Chelsea, London, greets Nigel Gordon, 3rd June 1965*)

(*Lawrence Ferlinghetti and Ginsberg in conference – observed by another Bard outside the Royal Albert Hall, June 1965*)

(*Ferlinghetti reading in Albert Hall, 11th June 1965*)

Allen Ginsberg Dying

Allen Ginsberg is dying
It's in all the papers
It's on the evening news
A great poet is dying
But his voice
                won't die
His voice is on the land
In Lower Manhattan
in his own bed
he is dying
There is nothing
to do about it
He is dying the death that everyone dies
He is dying the death of the poet
He has a telephone in his hand
and he calls everyone
from his bed in Lower Manhattan
All around the world
late at night
the telephone is ringing
'This is Allen'
                the voice says
'Allen Ginsberg calling'
How many times have they heard it
over the long great years
He doesn't have to say Ginsberg
All around the world
in the world of poets
there is only one Allen
'I wanted to tell you' he says
He tells them what's happening
what's coming down
on him
Death the dark lover
going down on him
His voice goes by satellite
over the land
over the Sea of Japan
where he once stood naked
trident in hand
like a young Neptune
a young man with black beard
standing on a stone beach
It is high tide and the seabirds cry

The waves break over him now

and the seabirds cry

on the San Francisco waterfront

There is a high wind

There are great whitecaps

lashing the Embarcadero

Allen is on the telephone

His voice is on the waves

I am reading Greek poetry

The sea is in it

Horses weep in it

The horses of Achilles

weep in it

here by the sea

in San Francisco

where the waves weep

They make a sibilant sound

a sibylline sound

Allen

    they whisper

        Allen

LONDON CROSSFIGURED

Lawrence Ferlinghetti

London

crossfigured
creeping with trams

and the artists on sundays
in the summer
all 'tracking Nature'
in the suburbs

It
could have been anyplace
but it wasn't
It was
London

and when someone shouted over

that they had got a model

I ran out across the court

but then
when the model started taking off
her clothes
there was nothing underneath
I mean to say
she took off her shoes
and found no feet
took off her top
and found no tit
under it
and I must say she did look
a bit
ASTOUNDED

just standing there
looking down
at where her legs were
not

But so very carefully then
she put her clothes back on
and as soon as she was dressed again
completely
she was completely
all right

Do it again! cried someone
rushing for his easel

But she was afraid to

and gave up modelling

and forever after

slept in her clothes

Michael Horovitz

Jeff Nuttall was a catalyst, perpetrator and champion of rebellion and experiment in the arts and society. *Bomb Culture*, his 1968 chronicle of the emergence of internationalist counter-culture in Britain, remains a primary source and manifesto for the post-Hiroshima generation.

The vision of Jeff's youth was grounded in "a faith that, given liberation, the human spirit would predominate. I imagined some kind of stone age village. People would build their own houses imaginatively and live there sophisticatedly and in a literate way, and they would live with their hands and their minds and they would not be dictated to by anybody selling them anything. People would have the opportunity of coming into their true self, which was generous and creative and permissive."

... Central to the burgeoning oral verse, jazz poetry, happenings and performance art movements, he also played effervescent jazz piano and scalding cornet in the Red Allen-Roy Eldridge idioms, and sang infectiously genial vocals. There were many sides to him. The humours of Fats Waller were recreated in Jeff's persona, yet he struck some, on a brief encounter, as an unrewardingly macho noisebag and show-off. For many others he was an outsandingly original artist also possessed of a special gift for helping countless fellow spirits to appreciate and fulfill their own potential.

Other precursors whose legacies he extended were the dadaists, surrealists and beats, Dylan Thomas, John Bratby and kitchen sink painting, McGill postcards, bebop and northern music hall. In 1967 he co-founded the People Show, an improvising theatre troupe with which Jeff travelled, wrote and acted for five years.

... In 1990 Jeff summarised his artistic approach: "I make a line out of a rhythmic figure. The previous figure suggests the subsequent one. The rhythmic figures owe much to Charlie Parker's saxophone phrasing." (A typical poetic example from the 1980s graces page 41 opposite).

... In Jonathon Green's *Days In The Life: Voices From The English Underground* (1988), Jeff recalled "a shift between 1966 and 1967 from poetry and art and jazz and anti-nuclear politics to just sex and drugs, the arrival of capitalism. The market saw that these revolutionaries could be put in a safe pen and given their consumer goods. What we misjudged was the power and complexity of the media, which dismantled the whole thing. It bought it up. And this happened in '67, just as it seemed that we'd won".

Nuttall lived to see that spirit rekindled 35 years later, with wise children again marching, speaking and acting out their hearts and minds against the philistines, profiteers and warmongers who go on ruling the west.

He died on Sunday 4th January on leaving the Hen and Chicks pub in Abergavenny, where his New Orleans revivalist band's lunchtime gig had been the highspot of his week for ten years.

At his soul's incarnation in Elysium it will surely come to pass, as Jeff once dreamed, that "Spifflicate water-buffalo drunk on rainbow fish will snore beside the oval father where he basks". For the rest of us, as long as "global politics" fester in lies and pea-brained Hollywooden mega-violence, it is bollocks to them, and long live Jeff Nuttall.

(— from Michael Horovitz's obituary of Jeff Nuttall in the Guardian, 12 January 2004)

Untitled

So brightly blisters the great regurgitating ribbon
                                    of the Thames
Sculls skim through like springtime swallows.
Keels kiss tidal scum, lancing the stolen sun-boils.

Echoes of these peppery explosions
Paint the ceiling of the Depot Wine Bar & Bistro
In a dancing manner of a watering,
Watering this way and watering that.

The Jab Bug can be heard from a distance,
Her twittering, her nesting-season-screams,
Her word-stabs.

The Jab Bug is so small and so appealing –
Her dawning innocence inciting hen-squawks.
The Jab Bug's cunt is not always as the running river of goodness.
                                    Just usually.

The glistening ribbon bends about the same way,
On the same elephantine curve.
The popping pods of spat light
Dither across the ceiling of the Depot Wine Bar & Bistro
And what the hell can a heart do
Yearning towards the blacker plums of love
But munch on the peanuts, the unusually shaped potato crisps.

Jeff Nuttall (1933 – 2004)

(Jeff Nuttall with Frances and Michael Horovitz in Gloucester Museum and Art Gallery, mid-1970s)

(Molly Parkin and Jeff Nuttall at the Cheltenham Literature Festival in October 1998)

Me And Jeff

The generous imprint of Jeff's final embrace lasted the afternoon and is with me still and shall be always. I saw it then as I see it now as the profound embodiment of everything that he and I had ever felt for each other.

We loved each other but were never lovers, we by-passed the exchange of bodily fluids, of saliva-strung kisses and passionate marathons. Strange to explain, but there seemed no need for all that. We were linked more powerfully, we sprang from the same soil and the recognition of that was there from the very start. To have made love to each other would have seemed uncannily incestuous.

But only we two fully understood the sublime pleasure we shared in each other's company every time we met. We quite literally fell upon each other, the reunion of twin-souls. Wherever it took place, in Soho or the Chelsea Arts Club, or down in my Welsh valley, the place of my birth. The joy was as pure and unadulterated as it had been the first time we ever met.

THAT FIRST TIME

MY HEART LEAPT
MY CHEEKS BURNED

MY MOUTH DRIED
MY THROAT CLOSED

MY KNEES BUCKLED
MY EYES SPARKLED

MY LIPS SMILED
MY SPIRIT SOARED

WE BURST INTO LAUGHTER
WHICH NEVER STOPPED

WHEN ME AND JEFF
MET THAT FIRST TIME.

I always took such relish from the look of him. Those rumpled curls and the roly-poly belly, reminders of Swansea's son, Dylan. The eyes of the artist. The gait of the jazzman. The tongue of the poet. The voice of the preacher. The chuckle of a cherub. All the elements were in place to create the captivating essence of the inimitable man/child.

I didn't fully comprehend when they told me Jeff had died. The blood drained out of my very bones. There was a sudden space in the world and I was feeling the draught. I didn't want to attend his Memorial Service in the church*, I would have preferred to grieve the sense of loss on my own. But I did go and was re-united with Jeff, all over again. Nobody had said that he would be there. He has been with me ever since and my life is immeasurably enhanced because of it.

"MOLL! Get off your fucking arse!" That's what he said to me there in the hallowed confines of the church, even whilst everyone was singing his praises. "Where are the WORDS? Write the BOOKS. Paint the PICTURES. Dance the DANCE. Listen to the JAZZ, girl!"

Yes, the imprint of Jeff's final embrace is still with me, alright. But the grasp and the grip of him is stronger than ever. I went to Mexico for the first time, a place we had spoken of together. And whilst I was there, in Mexico City this Spring, I wrote my first book in a decade and completed it in six weeks. Since my return, the paintings of Mexico have been pouring out of me. I renewed my membership at Ronnie Scott's, and every week I go to Paul Pace's basement jazz club at the Spice of Life in Soho. In Mexico I learnt the Salsa dance.

My gratitude knows no limits. The bond is deeper than it ever was. I now await further directions from the ether. The trust in my twin-soul has always been unwavering.

"My life is putty in your hands. I'll always love you, Jeff. But you know that, don't you, boyo."

Chelsea, 2005

(* – i e, the Wake for Jeff Nuttall in St John's Church, Waterloo on Mayday 2004)

And Then I Met Slim
(Poem for Slim Gaillard)

Smooching hours to Chet Baker,

Submerged in Monk,

Holiday for hangin' days,

Quincy to funk.

Stroke me with Vaughan

Wake me up to Ella,

Basie, Mulligan and Dexter

My Fellas.

Sublime in my ears

Fats to my heart

Give my body all up

To Gershwin and Reinhardt.

And then I met Slim,

Giant amongst men.

Those big brown hands covering

Keys, seas and souls,

Matched the chocolate voice

Dripping with Joy.

Too delighted with Dunkin' Donuts

and Cement Mixers

To trawl for lost misery.

Your Smile – bigger than any crescent moon,

And how you laughed! Laughed and Danced.

1932 Jitterbug Champion.

Teaching Ronald Reagan to

Voutorooni, word perfect.

Siring one hundred children (never mine) .

Father of Legends, Father of Fun.

I miss you still, Slim.

I miss you still.

Greasy Spoon

steak knife rusty, ketchup crusty, crispy bacon, greasy spoon
gristle wrapped in greaseproof napkin, oily mushrooms, greasy spoon
mother's pride deep-fat fried, greasy spoon, greasy spoon

photo-preview drip-proof menu, crispy bacon, greasy spoon
corned beef hash day, tin foil ashtray, oily mushrooms, greasy spoon
coffee dregs, rubber eggs, greasy spoon, greasy spoon

pepper powdered, green veg chowdered, crispy bacon, greasy spoon
sunnyside up, old chipped teacup, oily mushrooms, greasy spoon
tea-dyed cloth, tasteless broth, greasy spoon, greasy spoon

Blues For Slim Gaillard

VRRT URGHH YBVLU
LBVRA OIVRR VRRTSEESHOOM
MUVRUM DYAIRGHH RTSEESHEENAH

BMAGHVAM VDOI JHERRT
VULV'BLOI GDJVEEM LEHARRM
NYAIRD NIRR VDIRR

Matzoh Balls

well-a matzoh balls — gefilter fish
best old dish I ever ever had
matzoh balls — gefilter fish
makes you order up a extra dish
matzoh balls — gefilter fish
really really really very fine
now you put a little horseradish on it and make it very mellow
because it really knocks you right on out

(oh, bring me a side order of matzoh balls now)

well-a matzoh balls — gefilter fish
the best old dish I ever ever had
matzoh balls — gefilter fish
it makes you order up a extra dish
matzoh balls — gefilter fish
with a little horseradish on the side
makes it mellow, makes it jello
mellow as a cello, boy
horseradish with matzoh balls!

Cement Mixer

cement mixer, putti putti, cement mixer, putti putti, cement mixer, putti putti

(poodle-da-skoodie, poodle-da skoodie, poodle-da-skoodie)

cement mixer, putti putti, cement mixer, putti putti, cement mixer, putti putti

(Re-beat . . .) . . . . Concrete!
First you get some gravel,
(From the streams) about.
You mix a mess of mortar,
(Splash) a mess of water,
See the mello-roonie come out!
Slurp, slurp, slurp

cement mixer, putti putti, cement mixer, putti putti, cement mixer, putti putti

who wants a bucket of cement?

Black and White

Sitting with my friend Stella
In a parked car, on a hot summer day,
In the segregated city of St Louis
With Oscar Peterson
And bass player Al McKibbon
Two white girls and two black musicians

Across the street, staring our way,
Three big, sweaty, white men.
We stayed shtum
When they crossed the street as one
And leaned hairy arms
On the windows of our car.
Then one of them cleared his throat.
'Mr Peterson,' he said,
'Could I have your autograph?'

Snapshots

Photographs are smiles that last forever
Snowmen that can never melt away
Birthday celebrations caught in amber
Rescued from the vaults of yesterday

Faces that were once more dear than diamonds
Boys who kept you up until the dawn
Houses filled with bicycles and babies
Ghosts who left their shadows on the lawn

Then turn the page
And see the children grow
The adults age
The lovers come and go

Photographs are holes in time's grey curtain
Through them we can peek into the past
Call upon our parents and our children
Pop a cork with members of the cast

There they are, the days of jazz and joy-rides
Snaps of magic moments lit by laughs
If you ever find my house on fire
       Leave the silver
       Save the photographs

Fran Landesman

A Paradox

It's the happy memories
That make you sad
The awful ones
Are not so bad
You're looking back on
An illness cured
A love affair that fell apart
But you endured
And turned it into Art

It's the memory of a better day
So fair and far away
That breaks your heart.

Scars

Don't be ashamed
Everybody's got scars
From our various wars
On the way to the stars

Don't try to hide
Everybody's got scars
From crashlanding on Mars
With these egos of ours

There's the one on your knee
Where you fell off your bike
Or the bite from a babe
that you love but don't like

Theres the mess that you made
without counting the cost
Or the cut from a blade
Or the child that you lost

Don't be ashamed
If you're covered with scars
On this planet of ours
That's the way we keep scores

So I'll show you my scars
If you show me yours
In the streets and the bars
Everybody's got scars

On their way to the stars
Everybody's got scars

DICK HECKSTALL-SMITH

It's hard for me to write about Dick now, though I wrote about him when he was alive. We were close, and watching him die for a year still causes pain. Things I've tried to write since haven't come out right. Dick had become something of a crusade for me and it's hard to lose that kind of battle.

I grew up worshipping the great musicians of jazz, soul and rhythm and blues. Their tenacity in the struggle against commerce, racism and ageism was inspiring. Often disadvantaged, they felt more authentic than most other writers or artists. When one was lost, I took it personally, even if sometimes it was their own fault.

I supported Dick because I felt he was a truly great musician and individual, maybe the Brit equivalent of a Coleman Hawkins or Sonny Rollins; the main difference being that they lived in the Land of Opportunity and he was stuck here.

Nevertheless I got him deals and got his records made, and they were his best records, the ones that represented him; *Woza Nasu, Celtic Steppes*, and *Blues and Beyond* didn't sell so well, and Dick didn't get rich or much better known (except briefly in the U.S. where he was nominated for a W.C. Handy award for *Blues*). But they made a big difference to his later years, and there are a lot of young musicians who swear by them.

I first saw Dick play with Sandy Brown at the St Martin's Art School dance in '57. Sandy's band was no slavish New Orleans Revival copy or empty Dixieland, but blended African influences with swing and a little bebop. It was probably the first World Music band, something Dick was not slow to grasp.

When Dick joined Mike Horovitz and myself in the New Departures group, we were really lucky to have someone who understood poetry as much as he did. Although some of our communication was frustrated by the inadequate sound equipment of the time, Dick always seemed to hit the spot, both with his timing and his contributions to the atmosphere of a piece. With Dick and Graham Bond in the group, some very interesting freedoms were explored.

By the time Live New Departures got its Tuesday residency at the old Marquee Club in '63, Dick was making the beginning of a proper living working with Alexis Korner's Blues Incorporated, who had the Thursday night spot at the same venue. The ND jazz/poetry team moved more towards hardbop (with some free excursions) with the likes of Stan Tracey, Bobby Wellins, Jeff Clyne and Les Condon.

After Alexis came the illustrious Graham Bond Organization, by my reckoning the best U.K. band of the '60s. Dick's (and Graham's) entry into R & B was prompted by a) trying to earn a proper living, b) a love of the blues, and c) their non-acceptance by what had become the British bebop establishment, centred on Ronnie Scott's club. The boppers were largely ex-danceband players headed towards conservatism whereas Dick was ex-public and progressive school and a fierce socialist.

During the missionary New Departures years (1959–66), Dick and I became fast friends. When I was young and green I trusted his advice, musical and otherwise. Strangely, when he was older, he came to trust me in the same way.

Dick was responsible for big changes in my life; through him, I met Graham, Jack Bruce and Ginger Baker, resulting in my songwriting work for Cream, and the reason I live in a house. He also co-produced my first record as a fledgeling singer, managing to head off some of my manager's production concepts.

Later on Dick got me involved in writing for Colosseum, his 1968 band with Jon Hiseman, and his first solo project, 1972's *A Story Ended*. For the latter Dick's plan was to set a T.S. Eliot piece derived from Shakespeare's *The Tempest* to music, but the Eliot estate wasn't having any. Dick turned to me to rewrite it, and I'm still really proud of the result. I read it at Dick's funeral.

After his first marriage ended, Dick lived with me for a time in a flat in Montagu Square, and one night he played me a very soulful live version by Colosseum of the Bruce/Brown song 'Theme for an Imaginary Western'. I told him that the song had been written with him in mind, portraying the Graham Bond Organisation as a mixture of pioneers and outlaws.

When Dick had his near-death experience during his heart bypass op, he had to learn to play again, and I listened to him doing it in my basement, as the law students below his flat objected. Eventually, incredibly, he could play better than he had done before. It was around this time that I began working seriously as a producer, and co-produced all his subsequent records with Dick's longtime flatmate and keyboard player (currently in my own band) Dave 'Munch' Moore.

It was a horrible irony that Dick, who had been struggling for so long, had begun to get better paid work with the likes of the British Blues Allstars, just as his health declined. He played one of his last gigs with them in a wheelchair.

Yet on his final gig with Eddie Martin's band in Bristol he played great, never short of breath, invention or wit. He was just running out of life.

On my basement wall he wrote: 'All musicians think they're crap. Any musician who doesn't think he's crap, is crap.'

Once in the early sixties he had a gig with a local semi-pro rhythm section in Cambridge. When I asked him how it went, he said, 'Well, I was right'.

August 2005

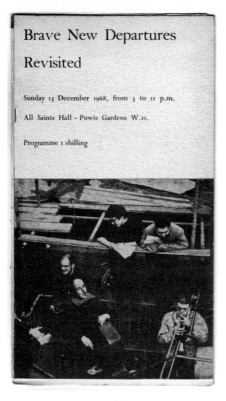

A vintage Live New Departures jazz poetry troupe: Laurie Morgan, Dick Heckstall-Smith, Shakespeare on bass, Michael Horovitz, Pete Brown and John Mumford outside the Cafe des Artistes, Redcliffe Gardens, in the late 1960s

from Urbano Blue

(healing shout for Dick Heckstall-Smith)

> ... blues
seeing the 16
year old woman
turning tricks
guts growling hungry
for a taste of smack
> blues
like the hole
in a rich
girls' shoe
as she flashes
the gold card
> blues
when guts and
brains is all
we've got or
will ever see
us through
> blues
of the river
at the end
of the street
open to the sky
like a wound
> blues
in this
strange country
that gives the
man it nourishes
both splendour and misery
> blues
when summer's ending
and all those questions never asked
in the moonlight
night
> blues
as every path
is not easy
to tread in
grace and
in danger
> blues ...

```
        . . . blues
of clear sharp
skies that make
the hi-rise blocks
on the horizon
look so clean
            blues
in the density
of population
and the filthy
back streets
because they're alive
        blues . . .


        . . . blues
on the concrete
slab platform
cold metallic
after the
rain
            blues
when you never
showed your
face but
judged me just
the same
        blues . . .
```

poem for D H-S

```
gobsmacking
spittle rasp
of a breath
down a horn
air gulp hiss
in a smatter
of arpeggios
tongue jelly
licking the scales
dick heckstall-smith
devours the stage
```

Reggae Sounds

Shock-black-bubble-doun-beat bouncing
rock-wise tumble-doun soun music
foot-drop find drum blood story
bass history is a moving
           is a hurting black story

Thunda from a bass drum sounding
lightning from a trumpet and a organ
bass and rhythm and trumpet double-up
team-up with drums for a deep doun searching

Rhythm of a tropical electrical storm
(cooled doun to the pace of the struggle)
flame-rhythm of historically yearning
flame-rhythm of the time of turning
measuring the time for bombs and for burning

Slow drop. make stop. move forward.
dig doun to the root of the pain
shape it into violence for the people
they will know what to do they will do it

Shock-black bubble-doun-beat bouncing
rock-wise tumble-doun soun music
foot-drop find drum blood story
bass history is a moving
           is a hurting black story

Phytoremediation

Do they gasp for air?
Pores choking on metallic dust
          for the lack of ozone–

Or do they choke on the idea
          of excessive ozone
in mixed up atmostpheres?

Bees crawl across their faces.

Do they gasp in pain?

Or is it joy? Are they drunk on sunlight,
          drunk on blue air?

Their greens and yellows reeling with the wind–

     These sunflowers, so tall, almost gawky,

          they are faster than Death.

     Undemanding queens–   What do they know?

Spartan beauties, I call them, sisters
of cacti, for they need so little almost
      nothing from the soil.

Do they never tire of looking at the sun?

The sun over Chernobyl,
for example, where they live—
roots soaking up radioactive uranium—
            stems humming radioactive cesium,
      radioactive strontium— a chemical heat
buzzing with zeros—

What do they mean with their glances?
Their electric, burning glances—
                  still beseeching bees,
still daring birds to eat their sees,
                  still glaring at the sky—
Still egging on the sun—

Ah! Sunflower

Ah! Sunflower, weary of time,
Who countest the steps of the sun;
Seeking after that sweet golden clime
Where the traveller's journey is done;

Where the Youth pined away with desire,
And the pale virgin shrouded in snow,
Arise from their graves, and aspire
Where my Sunflower wishes to go!

William Blake

from **Milton, Book 2, Plate 31**

Thou percievest the Flowers put forth their precious Odours!
And none can tell how from so small a center comes such sweets
Forgetting that within that Center Eternity expands
Its ever during doors, that Og & Anak fiercely guard.
First eer the morning breaks joy opens in the flowery bosoms
Joy even to tears, which the Sun rising dries; first the Wild Thyme
And Meadow-sweet downy & soft waving among the reeds.
Light springing on the air lead the sweet Dance: they wake
The Honeysuckle sleeping on the Oak: the flaunting beauty
Revels along upon the wind; the White-thorn lovely May
Opens her many lovely eyes: listening the Rose still sleeps
None dare to wake her; soon she bursts her crimson curtaind bed
And comes forth in the majesty of beauty; every Flower:
The Pink, the Jessamine, the Wall-flower, the Carnation
The Jonquil, the mild Lilly opes her heavens: every Tree,
And Flower & Herb soon fill the air with an innumerable Dance
Yet all in order sweet & lovely, Men are sick with Love!

I laid me down upon a bank,
Where Love lay sleeping;
I heard among the rushes dank
Weeping, weeping.

Then I went to the heath and the wild,
To the thistles and thorns of the waste;
And they told me how they were beguiled,
Driven out, and compelled to be chaste.

The Garden Of Love

I went to the Garden of Love,
And saw what I never had seen;
A Chapel was built in the midst,
Where I used to play on the green.

And the gates of this Chapel were shut
And "Thou shalt not," writ over the door;
So I turned to the Garden of Love
That so many sweet flowers bore.

And I saw it was filled with graves,
And tombstones where flowers should be;
And priests in black gowns were walking their rounds,
And binding with briars my joys and desires.

The Tyger

Tyger! Tyger! burning bright
In the forests of the night,
What immortal hand or eye
Could frame thy fearful symmetry?

In what distant deeps or skies
Burnt the fire of thine eyes?
On what wings dare he aspire?
What the hand dare sieze the fire?

And what shoulder, & what art.
Could twist the sinews of thy heart?
And when thy heart began to beat,
What dread hand? & what dread feet?

What the hammer? what the chain?
In what furnace was thy brain?
What the anvil? what dread grasp
Dare its deadly terrors clasp?

When the stars threw down their spears,
And watered heaven with their tears,
Did he smile his work to see?
Did he who made the Lamb make thee?

Tyger! Tyger! burning bright
In the forests of the night,
What immortal hand or eye
Dare frame thy fearful symmetry?

The Tyger is one of the perennially inspiring Blake lyrics I love singing with the William Blake Kezmatrix, a new group I have formed with trombonist-composer Annie Whitehead, pianists Tony Jackson and Pete Lemer, flautist Madeline Solomon and saxophone prodigy Michael Lukes.

This poem's sustained and mesmerising drumbeat rhythm, its immaculate simplicity masking infinite profundity, and its luminously physical imagery and music represent, for me, a timeless wake-up call to our shared humanity divine.

Each of the poem's twelve couplets speaks volumes and offers a peephole to the inexhaustible kaleidoscope of creative incentives at hand. For instance, "*When the stars threw down their spears / And watered heaven with their tears*" could easily be applied to our latter-day arrogantly self-appointed 'Star Warriors': If they were to pull all the way out of their currently massive and lethal arms investments, the resulting global sea-change would surely revive what is left of homo sapiens to "*smile his work to see*"; and so forth.

But the lyric is just as pregnant with the most immediate of gut understandings – as witness that of the 12 year-old schoolboy who, on being asked why Blake describes the tiger as "*burning*", thought about it for a moment, and then replied "Because it captures, er . . . the tiger's whole way of life".

– M H

William Blake Says: 'Every Thing That Lives Is Holy'

"Long live the Child
Long live the Mother and Father
Long live the People

Long live this wounded Planet
Long live the good milk of the Air
Long live the spawning Rivers and the mothering Oceans
Long live the juice of the Grass
and all the determined greenery of the Globe

Long live the Elephants and the Sea Horses,
the Humming-Birds and the Gorillas,
the Dogs and the Cats and Field-Mice –
all the surviving Animals
our innocent Sisters and Brothers

Long live the Earth, deeper than all our thinking

we have done enough killing

Long live the Man
Long live the Woman
Who use both courage and compassion
Long live their Children"

Adrian Mitchell

For Adrian Mitchell at 70

Michael Horovitz

Pied piper, loved mentor,
Blake child, firebrand,
War hater, peace planter

—Adrian! thou art living at this hour
Thank fuck.
Your care for every beast and flower
Is our good luck.

Where would Albion's Muse be today
Without you?
—Still stuck
In the nothing-new
Pseudo-intellectual prison
of an exam room without a view.

So keep on keeping on
True horseman
With the sainted Celia* at your side,
And however dread the nightmares
Go on schooling us to ride

Keep runing out the songs
And the poems and the plays
That map the concrete ways
To fight, and overcome the wrongs.

> "Poetry
> glues your soul together
> Poetry
> wears dynamite shoes
> Poetry is
> the spittle on the mirror" **

—Yea! Your life's work
Lifts us up,
Up and athwart
All those creeping
Heartless, mindless
Ill-willed, No-hope
Blue-oo-ues . . . . . .

* Celia is Adrian's wife and muse of 40 years, who also turned 70 in 200?
** — from Adrian Mitchell's 'Tyger: A Celebration of the Life and Work of William Blake', Cape 1971.

Adrian Mitchell

Live It Like Your Last Day
Dig What Can Be Dug

In the tunnel from Kennedy
the ceiling of metal or plastic
or plasticized metal or mettaled plastic
reflects the red tail lights
of a hundred moving automobiles

like a river of red light
I told my Albanian cabdriver
who never noticed it before

I said that's my job
noticing stuff like that –
I'm a poet

An upside down
river of red light,
he said laughing.

Now you're doing it,
I said.

Adrian Mitchell

Work To Do

As soon as I open my mouth and say
I'm a pacifist
A Political Person smiles and says:
Of course I respect your position – BUT –
Well, I say, I don't want your respect,
How about your Help?
Then the Political Person smiles and asks
The same stupid question time after time:
Wouldn't you have fought World War Two
To stop Hitler?
And I say No – and here's the reason why.
Because I wouldn't have fought World War One –
So Hitler wouldn't have come to power.
Sisters and Brothers
today we don't march out of fear or hatred
but because
we love each other
we love this beautiful planet
and all its wonderful creatures

we march out of love, in the spirit of peace
and whatever we do in the spirit of peace
is never wasted

we marched against the Vietnam War
in the spirit of peace
We didn't stop that war –
the Vietnamese people did that –
but we made it impossible
for British troops to be sent
to kill and die alongside our American allies –
whatever we do in the spirit of peace
is never wasted

for nearly fifty years we've marched
against nuclear weapons
in the spirit of peace
we haven't stopped the bomb – not yet –
but we have taught the world about
its terrible fate in a nuclear war.
And we continue to tell
the rogue nations of the world –

India, China, Pakistan,
Israel, the USA and Britain –
get rid of all your weapons of mass destruction now –
in the spirit of peace

we've marched together
we've sung and talked together
we've planned and argued and dreamed
and fallen in love with each other
oh whatever we do in the spirit o peace
is never wasted
and we meet today in the spirit
of William Blake who said that
 Everything that lives is Holy
in the spirit of
Mahatma Gandhi and Martin Luther King
and all their brave followers
we meet in the spirit
of the vast majority
of the people of this planet
who long for peace
whose deepest wish
is No More War
and whatever we do in the spirit of peace
is never wasted
So, like my Jamaican comrade
the poet Andrew Salkey used to say:
Brothers and sisters –
Keep on keeping on –
We've got work to do.

Adrian Mitchell

Slavery and War

The planet Earth in 1787 A.D.
More than three-quarters of its people
Were in bondage of some kind,
Including serfdom and slavery.
80,000 Africans were chained and fettered
And taken to the New World every year.
There was no anti-slavery campaign.

On May 22nd 1787
Twelve men met in a London printing shop.
The campaign against slavery began.
There were slaves and free activists,
Quakers, atheists,
And men, women and children
Who loved freedom
They were mocked as wild, impractical dreamers.

They had no e-mail or TV,
No radio or telephones,
But they found ways of showing the world
The obscenity of slavery.
So they abolished
First the international slave trade
And then slavery itself.
It was hard work.
It took them about fifty years.
    Only fifty years.
Today we can use e-mail, TV,
Radio and telephones.
We can abolish
First the international arms trade
And then war itself.
It'll be hard work.
Might take as long as twenty years.

(Written after reading 'Bury The Chains – The British Struggle To Abolish Slavery' by Adam
Hochshchild, Macmillan 2005)

SPAM

I come from a long line of canners.
We canned pineapples, that was our daily grind.
My Uncle Sam canned SPAM.
Grinding meat was his daily grind.

My Father said, "I have no bikini at all!"
My Mother said, "I have no bikini at all!"
My Uncle said, "There is no Bikini Atoll."

In 1946, the Yanks dropped a series of nuclear bombs on an island in the Pacific
called Bikini Atoll.

The islanders were relocated to where there were no natural resources, but for
compensation the Yanks gave them SPAM.

My Uncle decided to change his name, while the Yanks changed his address, and
renamed him and his wife, Sam and Pam.
My Uncle said, "We're Sam and Pam, together we make SPAM!"

Here's a quote from Paul Theroux's 'The Happy Isles of Oceania':

> *"It is a theory of mine that the former cannibals of the Pacific feasted on
> SPAM because SPAM tastes like human flesh. 'Long Pig' is what they called
> a cooked human being in Polynesia. It is a fact that the people eaters of
> the Pacific had evolved or degenerated into SPAM eaters because of its
> corpsey flavour."*

On July 10th, 1969, on the bombing anniversary of Bikini Atoll,
my uncle Sam jumped into the meat grinder at SPAM.
It was Sam's way of bombing them back.

But the Yanks compensated Pam
with 300 cans of SPAM

The cans that might contain my Uncle Sam.

Michael Horovitz

from **A New Waste Land: Timeship Earth at Nillennium**

. . . Is not a reverence
for life – for all land, sea and air
the path Jesus struck,
      Shock and Awe Basher Bush,
      Trade and War Preacher Blair?

Have you no shame?
            How can you claim
to follow Christ
when your fame has spread
so many dark days and nights
          with more dead
across so many lands, from your hands

    – famed oily blood brothers
  who wreak so much hurt, loss and fright
  – dread of so many children and mothers
with your gospel of markets and self-righteous might
whose weapons ignite still more terror and plight
filling land, sea and air
with endless infection, bombs and despair?

"Love thy neighbour
         as thyself"
– NOT
    "An eye for an eye"

is what Jesus preached,
    Big Top Barker Bush,
             and your yapping
    Dog-collared Upsucking
         Mascot Blair –

THE NEO-CRUSADERS

Our Cassandra

Still our Cassandra continues
to scream her truth,
each catastrophe coming
through the caul of her vision

Each catastrophe running
the gauntlet of her tongue
only to fall on   the walls
of disbelief and disapproval

Helen. A launching of ships.
Greek gifts.
Her sea-resounding voice
picked up by the ears

Of my own middle passage.
My own ships bowing
in prayer across Atlantic.
Her see-far eyes, like mine

Discerning everything –
from those suicidal Carib leaps
down to the soft massacre at Jonestown –
All the bloody reincarnations of history.

Her spirit-shrieks. My global shudders.
Her poor mother: *'For godsake girl,
spare me these endless gloomy prophecies
these visions of crumbling towers.'*

Angel Of The North

Travelling on an Intercity to Newcastle,
I spot you hovering somewhere over
Gateshead.

No cherubim or seraphim. No crossed swords
pointing to or from the great
northern forest

Just an angel emerging out of scrap-metal
and the conscience
of coal

Just an angel framed by sky and wind
guarding with corrugated
wings

The dark light of a people's spirit.

Wake Up And Hear The Music

(*God Speaks of Imagining Marty Robbins*)

And when the world began
I'd been asleep forever
I opened one eye
'Twas then it was I
Got the whim to wake

Wake up and hear the music.
Wake up and hear the music play.
Wake up and hear the music.
Wake up and hear what the people say.

And when the weight of space
Rolled like it was an ocean
One became one
Father and son
Watched the sunrise break

Wake up and hear the music.
Wake up and hear the music play.
Wake up and hear the music.
Wake up and hear what the people say.

And as the ocean warmed
And from this dream we woke
One sang to greet the dawn
One pursed his lips and spoke

I heard the heavens sing
Predicting Marty Robbins
I knew I'd find
Music and time
Were the perfect plan

Wake up and hear the music.
Wake up and hear the music play.
Wake up and hear the music.
Wake up and hear what the people say.

I watched my son sail on
A little ship a-bobbin
I had to grow
Needed to know
Exactly who I am

Wake up and hear the music.
Wake up and hear the music play.
Wake up and hear the music.
Wake up and hear what the people say.
Wake up and hear the music.
Wake up and hear the music play.
Wake up and hear the music.
Wake up and hear what the people say.

Pete Townshend

In The Ether

In the ether
I hang suspended
I wait for you
And I know you're near
In this high heaven
My world's upended
I feel no passion
I feel no fear

I'm dizzy with love
But you never appear
In the gloom of this room
Of this cell down here

I know this place
Isn't truly real
And that like my love
It expands and sprays
The light will find me
Will bend toward me
Yet I'm marooned
In a billion days

I'm drunk with you
And I can't explain
Who or where I am
Or how I'm in pain

Rocking and rocking me
Rhythm is shocking me
Just like a child in your fist
You are knocking me
Rocking and rocking
Autistic, caged I am
Rocking and rocking
And rocking enraged I am . . .

In the ether
I wait for you
Hanging in this mist
That I know's unreal
There is nothing there
There's no you, no me
Even though it's crazy
I still appeal

This is heavenly hell
I appear insane
I have no idea
Who there is to blame . . .

Around This Table

We built a home to live in
We love the things we found.
We fill it full of paintings
Put kelims on the ground.
Our friends all come to dinner
This table is our pride
We talk about the world's affairs
And those who've loved and lied.

We make love on it
Our children scratched their names beneath.
The fire lights our passion
And the wine has numbed our grief.
Then you bring other women
While I am out of town
And I can always sense
When a stranger has sat down.

Lots of pretty faces
Year after year,
Friends from all places
Have come here.
And we have spent a thousand days
Living in this room
And all who've been invited in
Still remain
Around this table.

Lots of pretty faces
Year after year.
Friends from all places
Have come here.
And we have spent a thousand days
Living in this room
And all who've been invited in
Still remain
Around this table.
We scream across the surface
Our hate is carved in stone
At opposite ends we fall apart
And I am left alone.

Well now you want this table
For your pretty mistress's home.
But ev'ry word will still remain
Eternally ingrained.

But I'll buy another
Where I'll entertain my guests
And I'll take a lover
To replace the seat you left.

Cigarettes And Housework

My teenage years were full of fear
I spent most of them inside.
Sitting on the telephone
Being bitchy and unkind.
Wandering from room to room
Trying to leave myself behind.
Walking with my eyes closed
Pretending to be blind.

Naked in the kitchen
I was smoking in the hall.
Vacuuming the sofa
Trying to make sense of it all.
Sweeping under the carpet
All my pain with all the dirt.
And the only thing that kept me sane
Cigarettes and housework.

Drowning all my sorrows
In an effort to be free.
Playing my piano
Writing a requiem for me.
Thinking I could clean up
All the trouble from yesterday.
Or hoping that my cigarette smoke
Would carry it away.

I have come through the trauma of youth.
But once in a while I still find myself

Naked in the kitchen
Smoking in the hall.
Vacuuming the sofa
Trying to make sense of it all.
Sweeping under carpet
All my pain with all the dirt.
And the only thing that keeps me sane
Cigarettes and housework.

Mohair

Green fields and brown walls
Enclose my garden in, and
Out the back on the hill is where I like to go
Though I'm told
there's wolves with teeth behind the brown
And sticks and stones to bring me down

When you were around I never went to tea
And now that you're not I don't know how to go
Past your house
Where there's things still there upon the walls
But there's not the sight of you at all

If you were here we could go dancing
The lot of us at the back of the bus
Red dresses on, down to the river for fun

If you were a bird
Would you sit outside her window
And watch her at night and keep her safe from woe
We miss you so
Oh reviens, reviens, ma chere amie
How could you leave so easily

If you were a bird we could go flying
And look below, wave at the folks we know
You forget these things when you're crying in church

So if you were here I'd take you dancing
The lot of us at the back of the bus
Red dresses on, down to the river for fun

Little Bigman

On the dark streets of a winter city
He showed me his big love to my face
By the time spring came I was still ripe and pretty
But there was another big girl in my place

My oh my, my oh my
That's how you make a big girl sigh
My oh my, my oh my
That's how you make a big man cry

He likes them big, oh he likes them singing
He likes them with their feet on the floor
He likes them dancing, changing tides, swinging
He likes them once then he doesn't like them anymore

My oh my, my oh my
That's how you make a big girl sigh
My oh my, my oh my
That's how you make a big man cry

He likes them big, oh he likes them sassy
He loves them like a dog loves a bone
Sadly for me he doesn't like them classy
Now my big broken heart has me crying on my own

My oh my, my oh my
That's how you make a big girl sigh
My oh my, my oh my
That's how you make a big man cry

Now then little bigman, if you'd have had the notion
For a little visit to a village by the sea
Well you could have been rocking in a big ship on the ocean
Going deep sea diving with me

In the sea, in the sea, in the sea
With the fishes and me
You should be sleeping with me
In the sea in the sea in the sea
With the fishes and me

Little Bigman goes a-walking
And the ladies start talking
Will you fall in love with me
He says, I don't think I can
Because I'm a coward
And I don't like mobiles
And the wife would kill me before we get to sea

He gave me his treasure
It was all in kisses
t was love me forever
But don't tell the missus
'Til inspiration comes to me
And the cold winds of the ocean
Sang the song of my devotion
To the land and the sea

From the big ship in the harbour
From the bandstand to the Tap and Spile
And all the way back to me
And the fish in the sea

  My oh my, my oh my
  That's how you make a big girl sigh
  My oh my, my oh my
  That's how you make a big man cry

You and me

You and me in a big white room
On a bed that goes on for days
Time and sunshine and a bottle of wine
Or more
Shut the door
Because that's what it's for

Rolling around, night can come soon
And night, you can stay til I'm done
I need to gaze on this lovely man's face
Some more
Shut the door
That's what my eyes are for

We would talk about music and agree with each other
You would look at my beauty and know
No more
Shut the door
That's what tonight is for

"It is not easy to be married."

Not Waving But Drowning

Nobody heard him, the dead man,
But still he lay moaning:
I was much further out than you thought
And not waving but drowning.

Poor chap, he always loved larking
And now he's dead
It must have been too cold for him his heart gave way,
They said.

Oh, no no no, it was too cold always
(Still the dead one lay moaning)
I was much too far out all my life
And not waving but drowning.

My mother was a fox.

Stevie

She laughs drawing scratchy pen women and cats.
She looks like any old lady dressed in an other time hat.
Walking down to the shops thinking of dead things that rhyme,
She's in another time.

You might see her over there
Stevie's not waving, but drowning.

Normal people in the park beat with monkey hearts
And she draws on them with cries and smiles.
And one day we'll all be done in, but it's more about the living.

You might see her over there
Stevie's not waving, but drowning.

They say that she's obsessed about death and that,
but what else do you laugh at?
While you live your life, she don't care.
She won't be possessed and that's why

You might see her over there
Stevie's not waving, but drowning.

Old Low Light #2

In a room banging on about the world in words
There's an old low light it flicks on and off
Like our opinions
Three hours without a word
Then you stroke my arm
There's an old low light in me
And it switches on

It's not visible to anyone but our love lives
There— I can feel it glimmer
It's slow and quiet and stares out at years
And it makes me love you more
More, more, more, more

In a different city bed in my sister's house
There's an old low light it keeps me awake
Without the shape of you
Track four on a CD you made for me
There's a note like light and it changes the air
And it makes me love you more
More, more, more, more, more

It's not visible to anyone but our love lives
There— I can feel it shimmer
It's slow and quiet and stares out at years
And it makes me love you more
More, more, more, more.

Beachy Head

Feels like I'm being taken over
And I know this isn't me
Feels like it's too high to get over
These waves just roll over me

Which way to go?
What happened to you?
Did you slip off the edge?
What happened to you?
Did you slip off the edge?

The sweetest sea air falling downwards
The sky arching like I'm trying to hold you
Ten sailors' pants could be cut from this sky of blue
Will anything take hold in you?

Training the morning to get up early
Asking the evening to get a good night's sleep
Wanting to change everything about me

chorus

Sweetest salty air falling downwards
The sky arching like I'm trying to hold you
Ten sailors' pants could be cut from this sky of blue
Is anything going to take hold in you?

What you really want is to fall upwards into the sky
Turn the world upside down
So you don't stop falling
So you never stop falling
So people will turn and say

What happened to you?
Did you slip off the edge?
What happened to you did you slip?
What a feeling inside
Pulling forwards pulling backwards
When are you going to fly
Will anything take hold in you
Will anything take hold of you
Will anything grab anything inside of you?
What's inside that stops
Anything holding onto you?

Love cuts

Love cuts
love juts out
and you walk right into it.

Love cuts
love comes and goes
love's a rose
first you smell the flower
then the thorn gets up your nostril
love gives you the chocolates
and then love gives you the chop
it doesn't like to linger.

Love cuts
love shuts up shop
and shuts it on your finger
Love cuts
what isn't very nice is
love leaves you in slices.

Love cuts
love's very sharp
a harpoon through an easy chair
a comb of honey in your hair
just wait until the bees come home
and find you just relaxing there.

Love cuts
love's claws
evacuate that heart of yours
and leave it on the sleeve it wipes
its nose on.

Love cuts, love guts the fish
of what you wish for
and leaves it in the airing cupboard.

Love cuts
love huts fall down
as all the walls get falser.

Love cuts
love struts around on stilts of balsa wood
love cuts love gives you a sweeping bow
then ploughs a furrow deep above your eyebrow
love cuts
love curtseys
then nuts you
where it really hurtseys.

'SO WHO IS THE FATHER, JOSEPH?'

Pop and me

My dad had come along to watch me
the day I came last in the cub scout sack race;
the day my glasses fell off on to the running track
and somebody behind me
deliberately hopped on top of them
and damaged them really badly.
I was that
struggling runt at the back
laughed at by everyone,
everyone, except my dad.
And not because he had
a beating in mind
but because he felt for me.
And when he came to find me
And I was melting with tears
he said 'You're the one
they'll remember in the years to come, son,
you were very funny.'
And he took me to the shop
and he ordered me some pop
and we halved the humiliation
when he didn't have the money.

Poet with bag

On A Yazoo Stem
(for *Michael Horovitz*)

Bespectacled bopper
for all rhymes and seasons
Squirrel hopper
gathering nutty poems
from Albion's unsung corners.

Runaway sunflower
climbing Blake's staircase
on a yazoo stem
grown-up still at play
with creepy-crawly friends

I have seen you in rush-hour haste
rucksackladen yet open to embrace
bearing that vulnerable aura
that mocks a mugger's fists.

Torch bearer schemer
of poetry olympics
not beyond elfish tricks
when the canon aims its metronome

But beyond the halo of eccentrics
and the zany loom you weave
the hasidic child is at home
under your colourful shirt

remembering holocausts
at nations' doorsteps
yet taking hope
in a hosanna of bay leaves.

WHO?

Whose Poetry Olympics are monster hits?
Who at the peak of Parnassus sits?
Who was born before the Blitz?
                    It's Michael Horovitz

Who shuns the glamour and the glitz?
Who wears tank-tops and home-made knits?
Who writes in longhand wearing mitts?
                    It's Michael Horovitz

Who's the scourge of pseudo-lits?
Who writes those fearless literary crits?
Whose Blakean vision is as clear as Schlitz?
                    It's Michael Horovitz

Who soars and sweeps but never flits?
Who's not afraid of Jesuits?
Who deserves a Knighthood and a suite at the Ritz?
                    It's Michael Horovitz

Who's one of London's sharpest wits?
Who plays the kazoo and has us in fits?
Who's the man we love to bits?
                    It's Michael Horovitz.

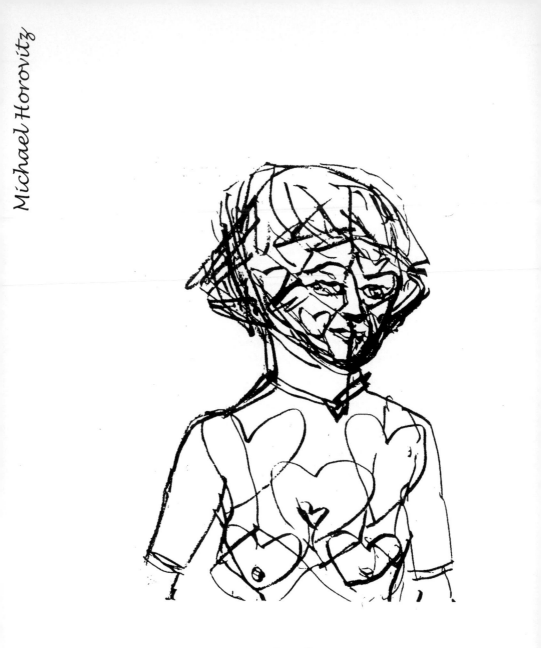

Love Poem

Self Portrait with Muse

Walking in Autumn

(for Diana Lodge)

We have overshot the wood.
The track has led us beyond trees
to the tarmac edge. Too late·now
at dusk to return a different way,
hazarding barbed wire or an unknown bull.
We turn back onto the darkening path.
Pale under-leaves of whitebeam, alder
gleam at our feet like stranded fish
or Hansel's stones.
A wren, unseen, churrs alarm:
each tree drains to blackness.
Halfway now, we know
by the leaning crab-apple;
feet crunching into mud
the hard slippery yellow moons.
We hurry without reason
stumbling over roots and stones.
A night creature lurches, cries out,
crashes through brambles.
Skin shrinks inside our clothes;
almost we run
falling through darkness to the wood's end,
the gate into the sloping field.
Home is lights and woodsmoke, voices –
and, our breath caught, not trembling now,
a strange reluctance to enter within doors.

Walking in Normandy

I walked for two hours under woods
cool as snowfall, filled with the encroaching
rustle of unseen hoof and tusk

and then the road bent out
into a valley blistered by daylight.
My legs dragged, swollen in the sudden heat.

Resting at a bridged-over ford, I watched
an otter flick past, its clumsy body
bullet-smooth under the water's tough skin.

It glanced through shafts of refractory light,
air bubbles burst above it –
a sound poem of recycled breath.

In the distance, tractors crooned under the weight
of sun-gorged sky. Even lazy insects
slowed their dancing along the stream's lip.

Leaning awkwardly on the bridge, I wished that I might
again be held in the river's crooked arm
transfixed, a bright otter at the edge of sight,

until cars passed, clattering like distant geese
through a balloon of dust. I rose; started the slow
stump home, apple brandy caught in my nostrils

Back to campfire and community
to the swell of tents, the maelstrom
of other people's children up past bedtime

all slipping crazily through the fire's fluctuating ambit,
their youth as luminescent and as brief
as bright bubbles of thought in the night's stream.

Song of Animals Dying

In a dream within a dream I dreamt a dream
of all the animals dying out
all animals everywhere
dying & dying
the wild animals the longhaired animals
winged animals feathered animals
clawed & scaled & furry animals
rutting & dying & dying
in shrinking rainforests
in piney woods and high sierras
on shrinking prairies & tumbleweed mesas
captured beaten starved & stunned
cornered and traded
species not meant to be nomadic
wandering rootless as man
All the animals crying out
in their hidden places
slinking away and crawling away
through the last wild places
through the dense underbrush
the last Great Thickets
beyond the mountains
crisscrossed with switchbacks
beyond the marshes
beyond the plains and fences
(the West won with barbed-wire machines)
in the high country
in the low country
in the bayous
crisscrossed with highways

In a dream within a dream I dreamt
of how they feed & rut & run & hide
how the seals are beaten on ice-fields
the soft white furry seals with eggshell skulls
the great green turtles beaten & eaten
exotic birds netted & caged & tethered
rare wild beasts & strange reptiles & weird woozoos
hunted down for zoos
by bearded black marketers
who afterwards ride around Singapore
in German limousines
with French whores

In a dream within a dream I dreamt a dream
of all the earth drying up
to a burnt cinder
in the famous Greenhouse Effect
under a canopy of carbon dioxide
breathed out by a billion
infernal combustion engines
mixed with the sweet smell of burning flesh
And all the animals calling to each other
In codes we never understand
The seal and steer cry out
in the same voice the same cry
The wounds never heal
in the commonweal of animals
We steal their lives
to feed our own
and with their lives
our dreams are sown

In a dream within a dream I dreamt a dream
of the daily scrimmage for existence
in the wind-up model of the universe
the spinning meat-wheel world
about to consume itself
And in a dream within a dream I saw
how the bad breath of machines
sickens earth and man
and consumer culture
eats earth and man
and bottom-line capitalism
masquerading as democracy
rapes earth and man

But in a dream I dreamt a dream of how
all the watershed people of the earth
all the ethnic peoples of the earth
all the disenfranchised people of the world
the Mom-and-Pop people of America
the youth of America and the poor of America
would at last rise up
and dismantle industrial civilization
without killing anybody
and save mankind from itself.

Wordsounds & Sightlines – New & Selected Poems

'Popular, experienced, experimental, New Jerusalem, Jazz Generation, Sensitive Bard' is how Allen Ginsberg characterised Michael Horovitz, introducing him to New York in 1970. Ten volumes of Horovitz's poetry were published between 1963 and 1979, when Growing Up: Selected Poems and Pictures 1951-1979 came out. Since then various pressures, notably his commitment to the encouragement of other writers and artists, stopped his more recent verse appearing in print, apart from the rural rhapsody Midsummer Morning Jog Log which was a Poetry Book Society Recommendation.

Wordsounds & Sightlines contains the poet's own selection of hitherto unpublished shorter pieces, as a companion volume and sequel to Growing Up. The new collection is made up of six sections: InterCity Poems; Light Verse; Songpoems & Lyrics; Homages & Updates (To Thomas Gray, Wordsworth, Matthew Arnold, Edward Thomas, Rupert Brooke, Joyce, Schwitters and E.J. Thribb); Elegies & Footnotes (for Beckett, Larkin and Frances Horovitz, among others); and Echoes & Transcriptions (of Bix Beiderbecke, Lionel Hampton, John Cage, rainfall at dawn, Beethoven, et al).

POP! (Poetry Olympics Party) Anthology

After the party...The Poetry Olympics Party Anthology includes the work of many of the people who attended the Party at London's Royal Festival Hall in April 2000, listed below. You can order your own copy! Simply xerox or tear off, complete and return the order form on page 112.

Featuring:

Ian Dury	Frieda Hughes
Julie Felix	Frances Horovitz
Allen Ginsberg	Harry Fainlight
Seamus Heaney	Thom Gunn
John Hegley	Gunter Grass
David Hockney	Carol Ann Duffy
Michael Horovitz	John Agard
Ted Hughes	Paul Weller
Jack Kerouac	Stan Tracey
Linton Kwesi Johnson	E J Thribb
Hanif Kureishi	Joe Strummer
Fran Landesman	Stephen Spender
Christopher Logue	Stevie Smith
Kathleen Raine	Damon Albarn
Brian Patten	Patience Agbabi
Grace Nichols	Beryl Bainbrigde
Moondog	Samuel Beckett
Adrian Mitchell	Jean 'Binta' Breeze
Shirley Manson	William Burroughs
Kirsty MacColl	John Cooper Clarke
R D Laing	Lemn Sissay

Midsummer Morning Jog Log

This 670-line rural rhapsody, Michael Horovitz's first book since 1979, takes the reader on a wildly exuberant poetic ramble round the Cotswold valley that was his home for 15 blissful years. The beautifully hand-set text is further illuminated by Peter Blake's illustrations, which redefine the pastoral 'magic realism' for which this artist has become so well known and well loved. The poetry and drawings together rejoice in 'every thing that lives' – above, beneath and beyond our intercity preoccupations (puff! puff!)

The 'ludicrously heavy-booted' author, once called 'incorrigibly urban' by Robert Graves, is seen as 'one of our more serious threats to the serious world' by Herbert Lomas, whilst Eric Mottram regarded 'Horovitz's need to deflate the pompous, to be immediately accessible, and to remind us of the childlike and naive as sources of freshness' as 'one of the most difficult ambitions in poetry. His strong appeal is: learn to recover your birthright.' This book logs the Minute Particulars of a summer morning's run on something of the scale of his earlier epic *Wolverhampton Wanderer* – but with all the visual, aural and imaginative delicacy of his more recent collections *Growing Up* and *Wordsounds & Sightlines*.

Writing about his work in the Literary Review, Herbert Lomas felt that: "There's something deeply English about Horovitz, as I understand the term 'English'. It's not just Blake, it's Smart and Clare and Samuel Palmer he lives with. I think his euphoria's a benign condition of hope, part of a seeker's happiness at an incommunicable message. Horovitz has moved out of ego-thinking and it's cost him the worldliness he'd have been very good at. To ego-thinkers it looks like irresponsiblity and goofiness, for they feel they're keeping society together only with stiff muscles and tight reins. We may feel threatened because Horovitz reminds us of our ambivalent, zany and ecstatic deeper mind that's longing to get out and induce the wholeness that looks like disintegration to the serious world of war and economic negotiation." These sentiments apply even more closely to the spirit and detail of Midsummer Morning Jog Log.

The poem is dedicated to the memory of Frances Horovitz, who first opened her husband's senses to nature at a deeper level.

POW! (Poetry Olympics Weekend) Anthology

An illustrated anthology of poets, singer-songwriters, musicians and performance artists of the world – to celebrate, commemorate and consolidate the first Poetry Olympics Weekend festival. Order this book using the order form on page 112. The POW! Anthology includes amongst many others,

Damon Albarn	Christopher Logue
Sujata Bhatt	Roger McGough
Nick Cave	Adrian Mitchell
John Cooper Clarke	Moondog
Ray Davies	Patti Smith
Carol Ann Duffy	Andrei Voznesensky
John Hegley	Heathcote Williams
Ted Hughes	Jah Wobble
Hanif Kureishi	Simon Armitage

(Poetry Olympics Marathon) Anthology

The POM! (Poetry Olympics Marathon) Anthology is a supranational galaxy of ascintillating verse, prose, song lyrics, art-works and photographs designed to rekindle the perennial torch of human fulfilment through the arts, and replenish the continuity of tenderness, good humours, beauty and truth, worldwide. Print out our order form and you can have your own copy!

Featuring:
Patience Agbabi, Beryl Bainbridge, Jean Binta Breeze, Claire Calman, Caroline Coon, Gregory Corso, Henry Fuseli, Allen Ginsberg, Duncan Grant, John Hegley, Anselm Hollo, Adam Horovitz, Frances Horovitz, Michael Horovitz, Frieda Hughes, Inge Elsa Laird, Fran Landesman, Christopher Logue, Paul McCartney, Adrian Mitchell, Jill Neville, Tom Pickard, Peter Paul Rubens, Lemn Sissay, Hank Wangford

Jeff Nuttall – Wake On Paper and On CD

A limited edition anthology celebrating the multifarious life and work of Jeff Nuttall, Polymath Extraordinaire, who died in 2004.

Also available – a companion CD featuring Jeff Nuttall on cornet and vocals, alongside such jazz giants as Coleridge Goode (singing bass), Lol Coxhill (soprano sax), Dick Heckstall-Smith (tenor and soprano saxophones), Ian Smith (trumpet), Martin Davison (clarinet), Jim Bray (bass), Peter Lemer (piano), and Pete Brown (drums) - in addition to ten supremely energetic spoken word and poetry tracks.

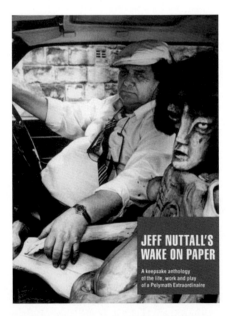

JEFF NUTTALL'S
WAKE ON PAPER

A keepsake anthology of the life, work and play of a Polymath Extraordinaire

Grandchildren of Albion – Anthology Voices and Visions of Younger Poets in Britain

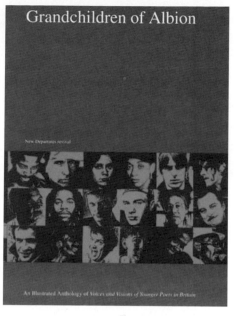

This lavishly illustrated 400 page anthology is the revival issue of New Departures (numbers 17-20), and has been described in the London Evening Standard as "crackling with more energy than the national grid", and in Time Out as "exemplary in its endorsement of multiracial work ... the essential buy for poetry lovers."

There are substantial selections from 40 poets, most of whom come to their most essential life giving readings, and/or projecting their texts in collaboration with various forms of music. They also relish connecting with each other and with every kind of audience, in multiple permutations, on the Live New Departures / Poetry Olympics bandwagons. Writers from the book available, singly or in groups, to give performances, talks, readings or jam sessions (and some of whom can also be heard on the Grandchildren of Albion Live CD and Cassette) include:

John Agard, Valerie Bloom, Linton Kwesi Johnson, Sujata Bhatt, Carol Ann Duffy, Neil Sparkes, Adam Horovitz, Jean Binta Breeze, Mahmood Jamal, John Cooper Clarke, Michael Horovitz, Stan Tracey, Ian McMillan, Ben Okri, Benjamin Zephaniah, Attila the Stockbroker, Grace Nichols & Keith Waithe.

Lost Office Campaign greetings card

All proceeds from sales of this card will support the Lost Office Campaign against the government's heartless nationwide Post Office closures and Royal Mail cutbacks.

The card features the 'Lost Office' poem by Michael Horovitz, with a centrefold spread of David Hockney's ink and watercolour painting of 'People in the Street', and satirical logos by Satpaul Bhamra.

Order Form

Name

Address

City   **Postcode**

Country

All prices include postage and packing.
Please send (enter number of copies required in brackets):

○ **The POT! Anthology**, edited and selected by Michael Horovitz
(112-page illustrated - ND 36-37 / ISBN 0-902689-25-8) at £8.99 each

○ **The POW! Anthology**, edited and selected by Michael Horovitz and Inge Elsa Laird
(108-page illustrated - ND 21-22 / ISBN 0-902689-17-7) at £7.99 each

○ **The POP! Anthology**, edited and selected by Michael Horovitz and Inge Elsa Laird
(128-page illustrated - ND 25-26 / ISBN 0-902689-19-3) at £8.99 each

○ **The POM! Anthology**, edited and selected by Michael Horovitz
(80-page illustrated - ND 32 / ISBN 0-902689-21-5) at £6.99 each

○ **Grandchildren of Albion Live on Cassette** (95 minutes - NDC 23 / ISBN 0-902689-15-0) at £8.75 each

○ **Grandchildren of Albion Live on CD** (78 minutes - NDCD 24 / ISBN 0-902689-16-9) at £11.50 each
(CD differs from cassette in that Ifigenija Zagoricnik-Simonovic's and Adam Horovitz's sets are omitted,
as are Donal Carroll's second and third poems.)

○ **Grandchildren of Albion Anthology** (400-page illustrated - ND 17-20 / ISBN 0-902689-14-2) at £11.49 each

○ **Midsummer Morning Jog Log**, 670-line rural rhapsody by Michael Horovitz
(Paperback edition, illustrated by Peter Blake - ISBN 0-9504606-8-0) at £4.25 each

○ **Wordsounds & Sightlines: New and Selected Poems** by Michael Horovitz
(160-page, cover portrait by David Hockney - ND 31 / ISBN 0-902689-20-7) at £7.74 each

○ **Jeff Nuttall's Wake on Paper**, edited by M Horovitz (40-page illustrated - ND 33 / ISBN 0-902689-22-3) at £5.99
e

○ **Jeff Nuttall's Wake on CD**, edited by Michael Horovitz (74 minutes - NDCD 34 / ISBN 0-902689-23-1) at £11.99
each

Lost Office Campaign Greetings Card, poem by Michael Horovitz and painting by David Hockney
(ND 35 / ISBN 0-902689-24-X) at £2 each, or £1

I enclose a crossed cheque/postal order for   to cover the total cost of this order, made

out to New Departures. Please send your completed order to:

New Departures / Poetry Olympics

PO Box 9819 | London | W11 2GQ | UK